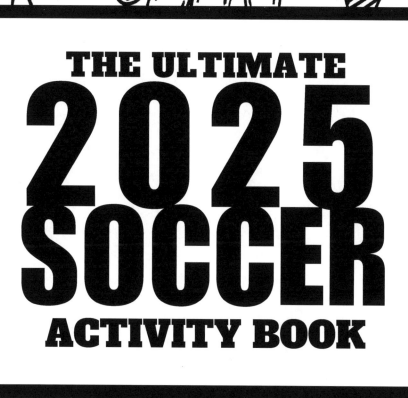

# THE ULTIMATE
# 2025
# SOCCER
## ACTIVITY BOOK

## FOR KIDS 6-12

### BRIGHT BALLERS PRESS

# INTRODUCTION

WELCOME TO THE 2025 SOCCER ACTIVITY BOOK! IF YOU'RE A SOCCER FAN AND LOVE TO HAVE FUN WHILE LEARNING, YOU'VE COME TO THE RIGHT PLACE. THIS BOOK IS PACKED WITH AWESOME ACTIVITIES THAT WILL CHALLENGE YOUR MIND, SPARK YOUR CREATIVITY, AND TEACH YOU COOL FACTS ABOUT THE MOST POPULAR SPORT IN THE WORLD—SOCCER!

INSIDE THESE PAGES, YOU'LL DISCOVER:

- MAZES THAT WILL HAVE YOU GUIDING PLAYERS THROUGH TRICKY PATHS TO SCORE,
- SPOT THE DIFFERENCE PUZZLES TO TEST YOUR ATTENTION TO DETAIL,
- COLORING PAGES WHERE YOU CAN BRING YOUR SOCCER PLAYERS TO LIFE,
- FUN FACTS TO BOOST YOUR KNOWLEDGE ABOUT THE GAME AND ITS LEGENDARY PLAYERS,
- WORD SEARCHES FILLED WITH SOCCER-RELATED WORDS HIDDEN FOR YOU TO FIND, AND MUCH MORE!

THESE ACTIVITIES AREN'T JUST HERE TO KEEP YOU ENTERTAINED—THEY'LL HELP YOU BUILD PROBLEM-SOLVING SKILLS, SPARK YOUR CREATIVITY, AND SHARPEN YOUR BRAIN. WHETHER YOU'RE TACKLING A TRICKY PUZZLE, LEARNING FUN SOCCER TRIVIA, OR ADDING YOUR OWN COLORS TO THE GAME'S BIGGEST MOMENTS, YOU'LL BE LEARNING WITHOUT EVEN REALIZING IT!

SO, GRAB YOUR PENCILS AND GET READY TO DIVE INTO THIS SOCCER ADVENTURE. IT'S TIME TO EXPLORE THE WORLD OF SOCCER IN A FUN AND CREATIVE WAY. LET'S KICK OFF AND ENJOY THE GAME!

# MAZE #1

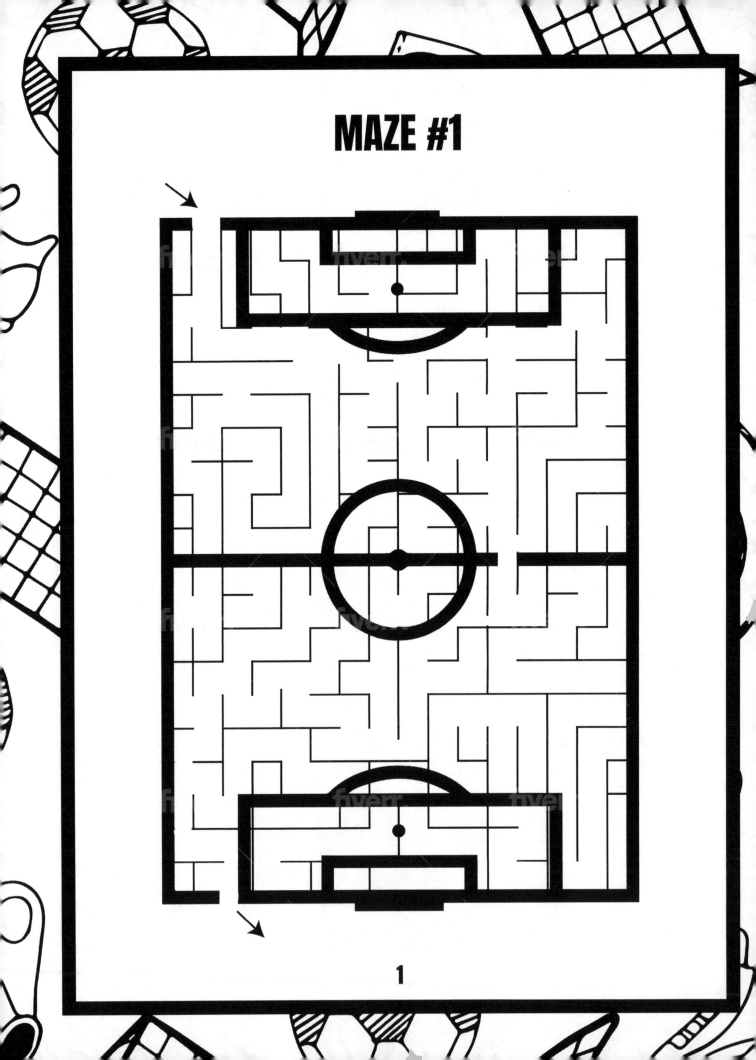

1

# THE NEW GENERAL MANAGER

## YOU HAVE BEEN APPOINTED THE NEW GENERAL MANAGER OF YOUR FAVOURITE SOCCER CLUB WRITE DOWN ANY CHANGES THAT YOU WOULD MAKE.

_____

_____

_____

_____

_____

_____

_____

_____

_____

**SIGNED** _____

# YOUR STATS CARD

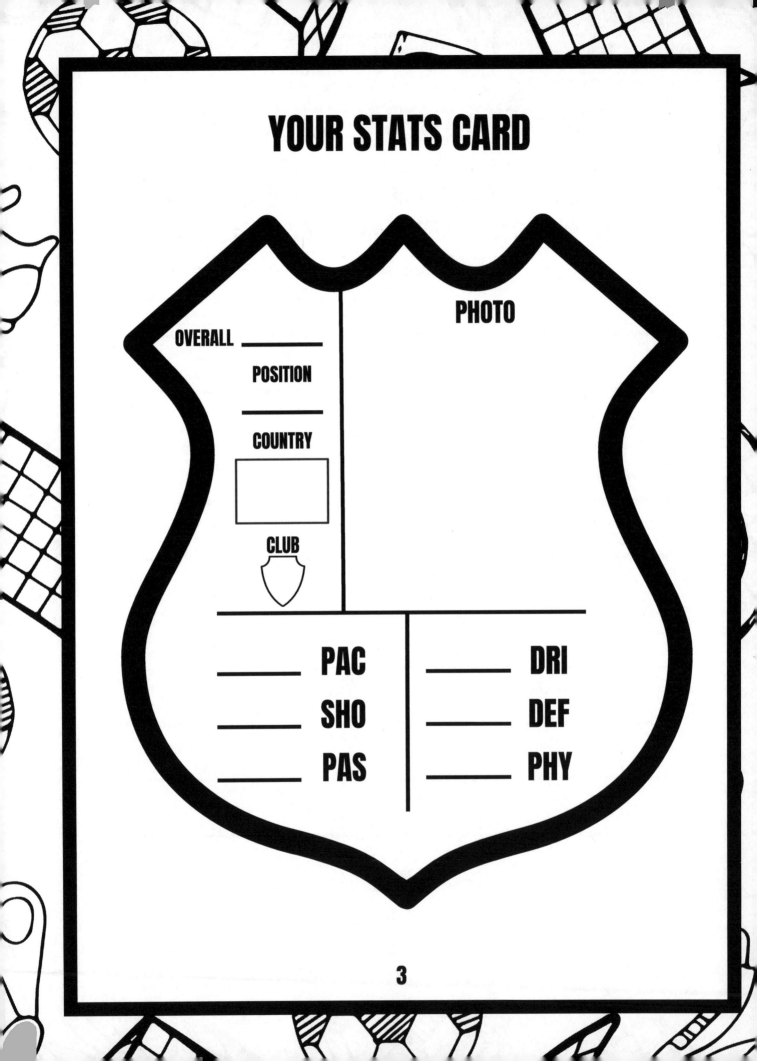

OVERALL _____

POSITION

_____

COUNTRY

CLUB

PHOTO

_____ PAC     _____ DRI

_____ SHO     _____ DEF

_____ PAS     _____ PHY

# SOCCER FACTS #1

THE 2025 AFRICA CUP OF NATIONS (AFCON) WILL BE HELD IN MOROCCO. EGYPT IS THE MOST SUCCESSFUL TEAM IN AFCON HISTORY, HAVING WON THE TOURNAMENT A RECORD 7 TIMES.

2025 MARKS THE 30TH ANNIVERSARY OF MAJOR LEAGUE SOCCER (MLS) IN THE UNITED STATES.

THE 2025 FIFA CLUB WORLD CUP IS SCHEDULED TO RUN FROM JUNE 15 TO JULY 13, 2025.

# DESIGN YOUR OWN JERSEY

# CREATE A CHANT

A SOCCER CHANT IS A SONG OR CHEER THAT FANS SING DURING A SOCCER GAME TO SUPPORT THEIR TEAM AND CREATE A FUN, EXCITING ATMOSPHERE. CHANTS ARE USUALLY SIMPLE AND EASY FOR EVERYONE TO SING TOGETHER. FANS USE THEM TO:

CHEER FOR THEIR TEAM AND MOTIVATE THE PLAYERS.
CELEBRATE A FAVORITE PLAYER OR A GREAT PLAY.
BOTHER THE OPPOSING TEAM TO DISTRACT THEM.

CHANTS ARE A BIG PART OF SOCCER CULTURE AND HELP FANS FEEL CONNECTED WHILE MAKING THE GAME MORE EXCITING!

HERE ARE SOME EXAMPLES:

YOU'LL NEVER WALK ALONE" - LIVERPOOL
"WHEN YOU WALK THROUGH A STORM
HOLD YOUR HEAD UP HIGH,
AND DON'T BE AFRAID OF THE DARK...
AT THE END OF A STORM, THERE'S A GOLDEN SKY,
AND THE SWEET SILVER SONG OF A LARK..."

BLUE IS THE COLOUR" - CHELSEA
"BLUE IS THE COLOUR, FOOTBALL IS THE GAME,
WE'RE ALL TOGETHER AND WINNING IS OUR AIM,
SO CHEER US ON THROUGH THE SUN AND RAIN,
'CAUSE CHELSEA, CHELSEA IS OUR NAME!

"YOU'RE NOT SINGING ANYMORE"
"YOU'RE NOT SINGING,
YOU'RE NOT SINGING,
YOU'RE NOT SINGING ANYMORE!"

CAN WE PLAY YOU EVERY WEEK?"
"CAN WE PLAY YOU,
CAN WE PLAY YOU,
CAN WE PLAY YOU EVERY WEEK?"

TO CREATE YOUR OWN SOCCER CHANT, PICK A SIMPLE, CATCHY TUNE (LIKE A NURSERY RHYME OR POP SONG) AND WRITE FUN, EASY-TO-REMEMBER LYRICS THAT CHEER FOR YOUR TEAM OR FAVORITE PLAYER. MAKE SURE IT'S REPETITIVE SO FANS CAN EASILY JOIN IN AND SING TOGETHER!

_____

_____

_____

# COLORING PAGE

# WOULD YOU RATHER #1

WOULD YOU RATHER BE THE FASTEST PLAYER ON THE TEAM OR HAVE THE BEST DRIBBLING SKILLS?

WOULD YOU RATHER SCORE A GOAL WITH A BICYCLE KICK OR A LONG-RANGE FREE KICK?

WOULD YOU RATHER BE THE TEAM CAPTAIN OR THE TOP SCORER?

WOULD YOU RATHER PLAY FOR YOUR NATIONAL TEAM OR YOUR FAVORITE CLUB?

# WORD SCRAMBLE #1

CAN YOU GUESS THE SOCCER UNIFORM ITEM.

**YESEJR** _____

**SCSKO** _____

**REGA** _____

**TSORHS** _____

**ASTELC** _____

# COPY THE DRAWING #1

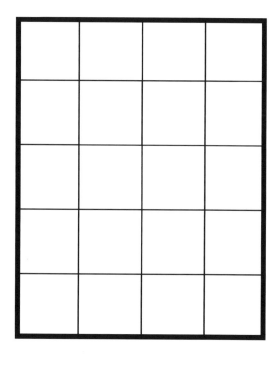

# RIDDLES #1

I RUN UP AND DOWN THE FIELD ALL DAY, BLOWING MY WHISTLE TO CONTROL THE PLAY.

WHO AM I?

_____

I PROTECT YOUR LEGS DURING THE GAME, SO YOU DON'T FEEL THE KICK OR THE PAIN.

WHAT AM I?

_____

I'M LACED UP TIGHT AND HELP YOU RUN FAST, I'M WORN ON YOUR FEET, AND I'M BUILT TO LAST.

WHAT AM I?

_____

# WORD SEARCH #1

```
Z U D Z V T L X D U L O N G I J
H D F N S V T M I V M L K R W E
P J P L J K B D T G N L E J F C
M D K U J F V W V G A P J E H I
Q W X S C Z Q Z Q O E H H R W A
P V N A Y X R I G E E O J S O Q
I I M U S T R I K E R Q K E J K
I W T S Y C H L L S N N G Y G Y
C I T C I K A P E N A L T Y T C
R Q U L H O W Z Z V R X D F S L
S J Q L G A B I F M W E Q X P E
F M H J P B B C Y E U K E E V A
K P Y E M T D Q C C X Q I R M T
N P A X K B S Z D V W R H Z S S
B N M K C P B S K M L S T U J J
G P Y C K X I M O P J Q O Z Z A
```

CLEATS
GOALKEEPER
MLS
PITCH

GOAL
JERSEY
PENALTY
STRIKER

# COLORING PAGE

# SOCCER MATHS #1

⚽ + ⚽ + 🧤 = 16. IF ⚽ = 6, HOW MANY IS 🧤 WORTH?

_____

🚩 + 🚩 + ⚽ + ⚽ = 28. IF ⚽ = 8, HOW MANY IS 🚩 WORTH?

.

_____

🧤 + 🚩 + ⚽ = 22. IF 🧤 = 5 AND 🚩 = 7, HOW MANY IS ⚽ WORTH?

_____

# MAZE #2

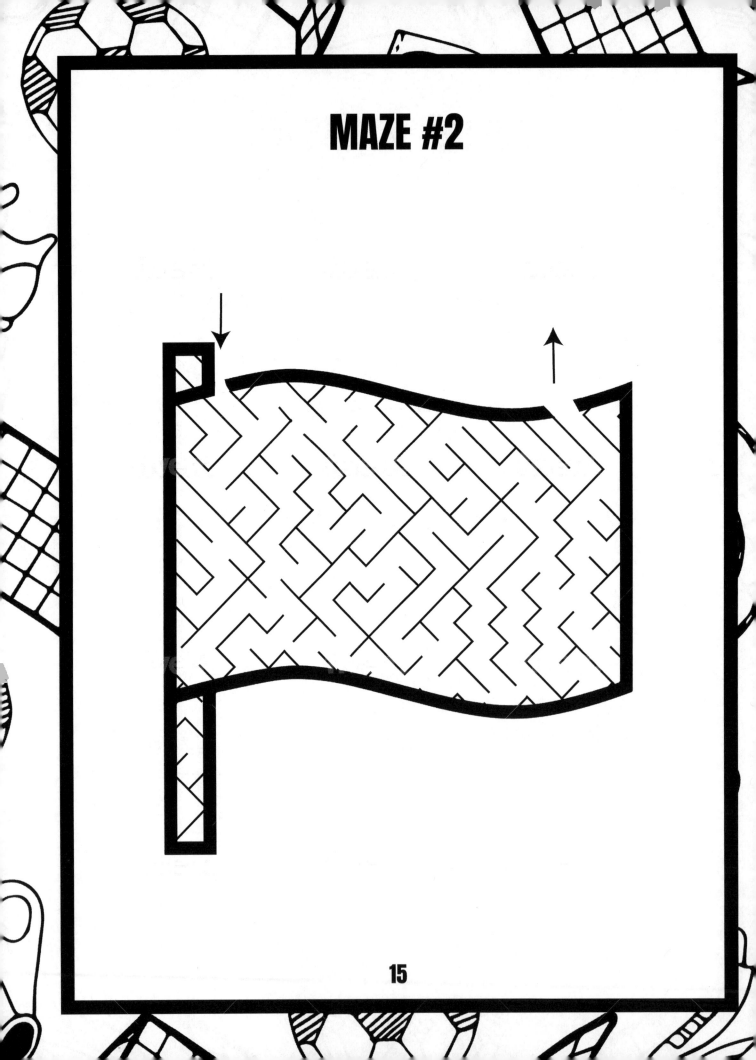

# GUESS THE FLAG #1

_____

_____

_____

# NAME 10 PLAYERS STARTING WITH B

1. _____

2. _____

3. _____

4. _____

5. _____

6. _____

7. _____

8. _____

9. _____

10. _____

# YOUR ULTIMATE SOCCER PLAYER

## NAME YOUR ULTIMATE PLAYER IN EACH BOX

INTELLIGENCE

HEADING

LEADER

STRENGTH

SPEED

ENDURANCE

SHOOTING

# SOCCER TACTICS #1

## SET UP YOUR TEAM TO SCORE A CORNER USING 'X' AS YOUR PLAYERS.

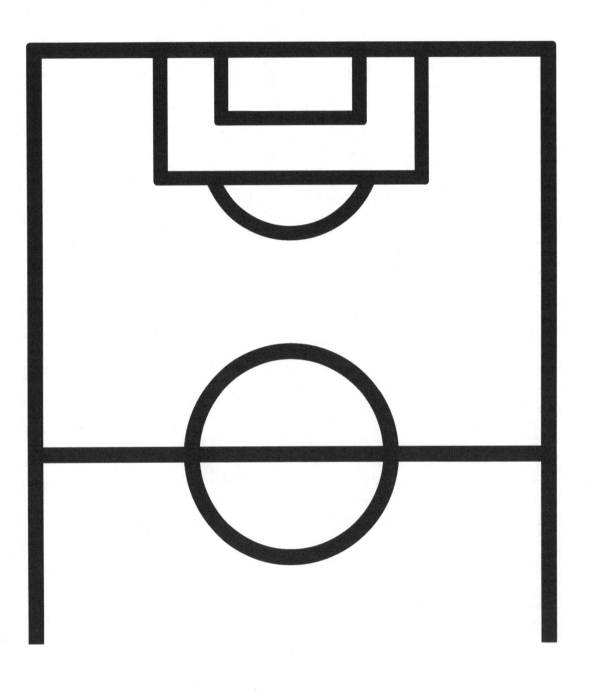

# SOCCER FACTS #2

MAJOR LEAGUE SOCCER (MLS) WAS FOUNDED IN 1993, BUT ITS FIRST SEASON WAS PLAYED IN 1996. THERE WERE ONLY 10 TEAMS AT THE START, AND THE FIRST-EVER MLS CUP FINAL WAS WON BY D.C. UNITED.

ONE OF THE MOST FAMOUS PLAYERS TO EVER PLAY IN MLS IS DAVID BECKHAM. WHEN HE JOINED LA GALAXY IN 2007, IT BROUGHT A LOT OF ATTENTION TO THE LEAGUE. BECKHAM'S MOVE TO THE U.S. ALSO HELPED PAVE THE WAY FOR OTHER INTERNATIONAL STARS TO JOIN MLS.

ARSENAL REMAINS THE ONLY TEAM TO GO AN ENTIRE ENGLISH PREMIER LEAGUE SEASON UNBEATEN. IN THE 2003-2004 SEASON, THEY FINISHED THE CAMPAIGN WITH A RECORD OF 26 WINS AND 12 DRAWS, EARNING THE NICKNAME "THE INVINCIBLES."

# HISTORY OF SOCCER #1

SOCCER HAS BEEN PLAYED IN THE UNITED STATES SINCE THE LATE 1800S. THE FIRST ORGANIZED SOCCER GAME IN THE U.S. TOOK PLACE IN 1869 BETWEEN PRINCETON AND RUTGERS UNIVERSITY.

FIFA, THE INTERNATIONAL FEDERATION OF ASSOCIATION FOOTBALL, WAS FORMED IN PARIS IN 1904 TO OVERSEE INTERNATIONAL COMPETITION AMONG NATIONAL ASSOCIATIONS OF BELGIUM, DENMARK, FRANCE, GERMANY, THE NETHERLANDS, SPAIN, SWEDEN, AND SWITZERLAND.

THE FIRST FIFA WORLD CUP WAS HELD IN URUGUAY IN 1930. URUGUAY ALSO WON THIS FIRST WORLD CUP.

WOMEN HAVE BEEN PLAYING SOCCER FOR AS LONG AS MEN HAVE, BUT THE FIRST RECORDED WOMEN'S SOCCER MATCH TOOK PLACE IN 1895 IN LONDON.

MAJOR LEAGUE SOCCER (MLS) IS THE TOP PROFESSIONAL SOCCER LEAGUE IN THE U.S., FOUNDED IN 1993.

# RIDDLES #2

I'M AN ENGLISH FORWARD WHO PLAYS IN GERMANY, I'VE WON MULTIPLE PREMIER LEAGUE GOLDEN BOOTS.

WHO AM I?

_____

I'M A POLISH STRIKER KNOWN FOR SCORING LOTS OF GOALS, I'VE PLAYED FOR BAYERN MUNICH AND BARCELONA.

WHO AM I?

_____

I'M AN EGYPTIAN FORWARD WITH AMAZING GOAL-SCORING SKILLS, I'VE WON THE PREMIER LEAGUE AND CHAMPIONS LEAGUE WITH LIVERPOOL.

WHO AM I?

_____

# MAZE #3

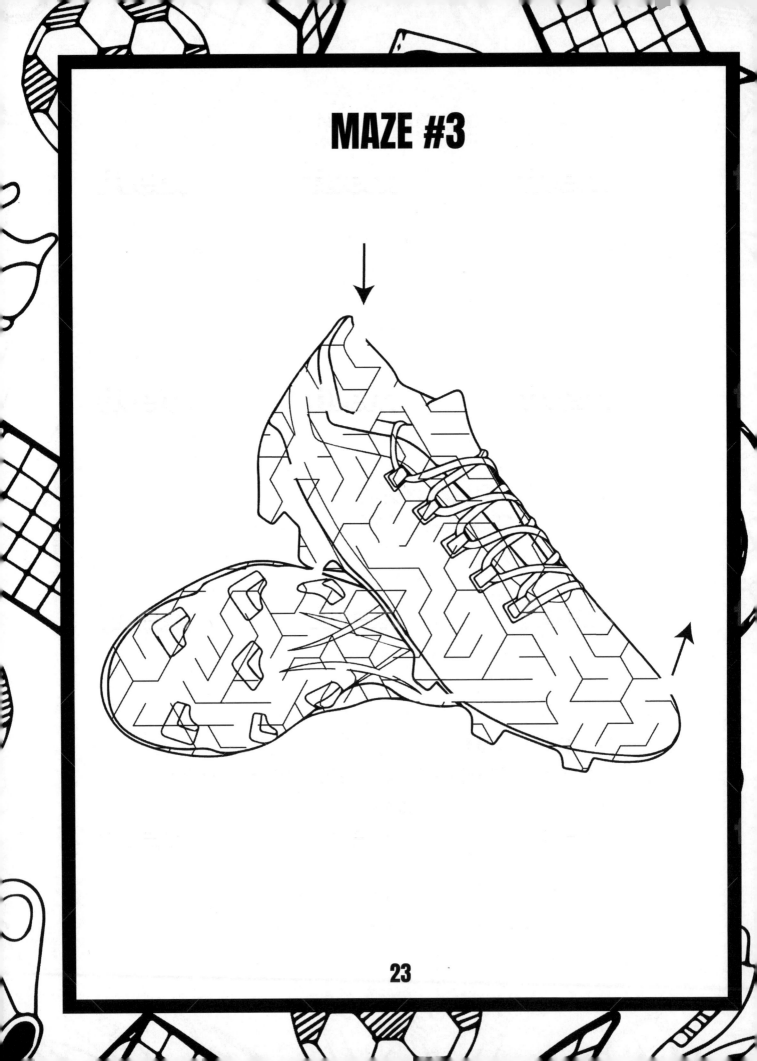

# WORD SCRAMBLE #2

## CAN YOU GUESS THE SOCCER TEAMS

**ANM INUDET** _____

**LEESAHC** _____

**LSAARNE** _____

**IERTN IMIAM CF** _____

**ERAL RMIDDA** _____

# SUDOKU #1

|   |   |   |   |
|---|---|---|---|
| 3 |   |   |   |
|   |   |   |   |
|   |   |   | 1 |
| 4 |   | 3 |   |

# SPOT THE DIFFERENCE #1

## SPOT THE 3 DIFFERENCES

# DESIGN YOUR OWN SOCCER KIT

# COLORING PAGE

# WOULD YOU RATHER #2

WOULD YOU RATHER HAVE AMAZING PASSING ABILITY OR INCREDIBLE SHOOTING?

WOULD YOU RATHER WIN EVERY GAME BUT NEVER SCORE A GOAL, OR SCORE IN EVERY GAME BUT NEVER WIN?

WOULD YOU RATHER PLAY IN A HUGE STADIUM WITH NO FANS OR A SMALL STADIUM PACKED WITH CHEERING SUPPORTERS?

WOULD YOU RATHER NEVER GET TIRED DURING A GAME OR NEVER GET INJURED?

# COPY THE DRAWING #2

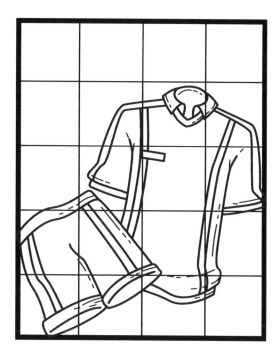

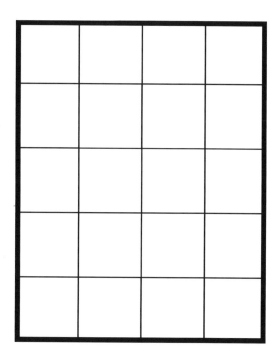

# YOUR FAVOURITE PLAYER

## 1. PLAYER'S BASIC INFO

PLAYER'S NAME: _____

TEAM THEY PLAY FOR: _____

POSITION: _____

NATIONALITY: _____

## 2. WHY I LIKE THIS PLAYER

WHAT MAKES THEM SPECIAL: _____

BEST SKILL: _____

MY FAVORITE MOMENT OF THIS PLAYER: _____

## 3. PLAYER'S ACHIEVEMENTS

NUMBER OF GOALS SCORED: _____

TROPHIES WON: _____

AWARDS (E.G., BEST PLAYER): _____

## 4. FUN FACTS ABOUT THE PLAYER

NICKNAME: _____

FAMOUS CELEBRATION: _____

SOMETHING COOL ABOUT THEM: _____

## 5. HOW THEY INSPIRE ME

WHAT I LEARN FROM THEM: _____

_____

HOW I WANT TO PLAY LIKE THEM: _____

_____

# WORD SEARCH #2

```
E  A  I  M  T  N  K  R  Z  I  I  W  L  P  F  A
R  Q  C  J  F  P  E  A  F  H  S  J  W  O  A  I
A  J  M  T  M  D  P  A  S  S  I  S  T  O  L  J
P  M  T  S  N  I  D  W  O  S  E  F  O  N  K  T
W  T  Z  E  S  P  D  F  Z  P  E  H  J  E  B  U
X  H  F  U  U  C  F  F  L  G  Y  O  L  J  P  R
N  E  V  M  B  O  U  Y  I  F  J  B  C  M  L  U
D  N  Q  C  S  R  C  O  U  E  B  F  G  Y  M  E
T  F  P  N  T  N  F  W  F  I  L  L  Q  H  R  C
R  P  G  T  I  E  Y  R  R  F  H  D  C  N  F  T
A  R  N  T  T  R  J  D  E  R  S  G  E  N  K  M
Y  T  R  H  U  K  Y  U  Y  E  D  I  R  R  R  Q
P  X  V  Z  T  I  W  L  T  D  K  R  D  M  Q  O
I  O  X  E  I  C  U  N  Z  A  K  I  P  E  W  E
O  H  Y  B  O  K  L  H  V  F  A  P  C  N  I  J
F  T  K  E  N  Q  R  N  E  Q  M  H  K  K  I  K
```

ASSIST
DEFENDER
FREE KICK
OFFSIDE

CORNER KICK
DRIBBLE
MIDFIELDER
SUBSTITUTION

# SOCCER JOURNAL

TEAM NAME: _____

MY POSITION: _____

COACH'S NAME: _____

FAVORITE TEAMMATE: _____

## HIGHLIGHTS OF MY SEASON SO FAR

BEST MATCH: _____

MY BEST GOAL: _____

TOUGHEST OPPONENT: _____

PROUDEST MOMENT: _____

## STATS OF THE YEAR SO FAR

GOALS SCORED: _____

ASSISTS MADE: _____

MATCHES PLAYED: _____

TROPHIES WON (IF ANY): _____

## FUN MEMORIES
BEST FOOTBALL MEMORY:

_____

FUNNIEST MOMENT:

_____

BIGGEST CHALLENGE:

_____

# NAME 10 TEAMS STARTING WITH M

1. _____

2. _____

3. _____

4. _____

5. _____

6. _____

7. _____

8. _____

9. _____

10. _____

# COLORING PAGE

# YOUR THE MANAGER #1

## CHOOSE YOUR ULTIMATE TEAM TO FACE A STRONG, PHYSICAL AND FAST TEAM.

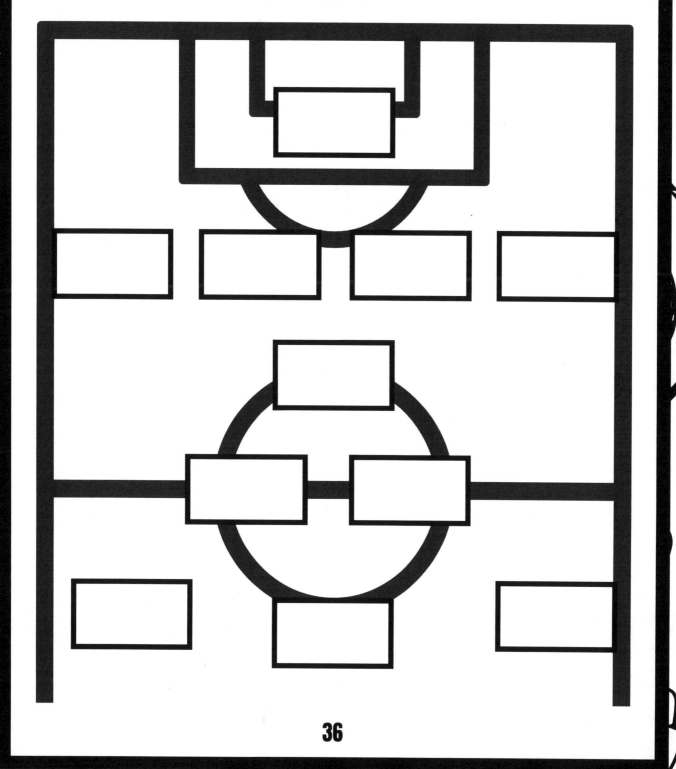

# DESIGN YOUR STADIUM

## COLOR IN AND DRAW THE SURROUNDINGS.

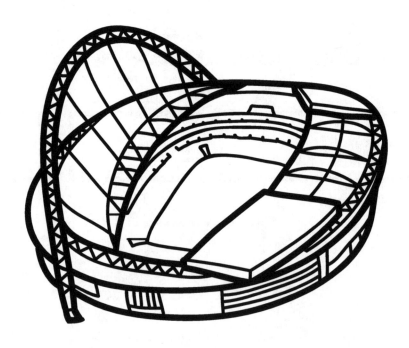

# MAZE #4

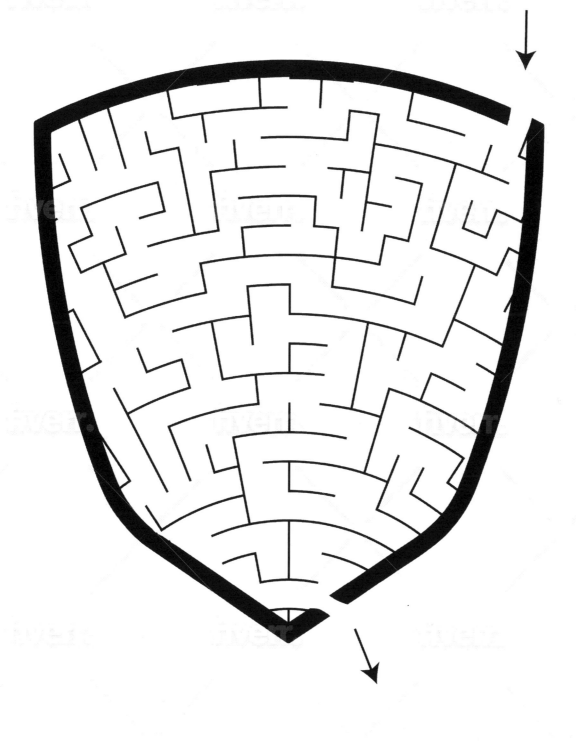

# PREDICTIONS

## MLS EASTERN CONFERENCE

| POSITION | TEAM |
|---|---|
| 1 | _____ |
| 2 | _____ |
| 3 | _____ |
| 4 | _____ |
| 5 | _____ |
| 6 | _____ |
| 7 | _____ |
| 8 | _____ |
| 9 | _____ |
| 10 | _____ |
| 11 | _____ |
| 12 | _____ |
| 13 | _____ |
| 14 | _____ |

## MLS WESTERN CONFERENCE

| POSITION | TEAM |
|---|---|
| 1 | _____ |
| 2 | _____ |
| 3 | _____ |
| 4 | _____ |
| 5 | _____ |
| 6 | _____ |
| 7 | _____ |
| 8 | _____ |
| 9 | _____ |
| 10 | _____ |
| 11 | _____ |
| 12 | _____ |
| 13 | _____ |
| 14 | _____ |

# SEASON CALENDAR

# WOULD YOU RATHER #3

WOULD YOU RATHER BE KNOWN FOR YOUR POWERFUL SHOTS OR YOUR INCREDIBLE DEFENSIVE SKILLS?

WOULD YOU RATHER SCORE THE WINNING GOAL IN THE FINAL MINUTE OR ASSIST THE WINNING GOAL WITH A PERFECT PASS?

WOULD YOU RATHER PLAY IN THE RAIN OR UNDER THE HOT SUN?

WOULD YOU RATHER PLAY ON A MUDDY PITCH OR A HARD PITCH?

# SPOT THE DIFFERENCE #2

## SPOT THE 3 DIFFERENCES

# RIDDLES #3

I'M A BRAZILIAN FORWARD KNOWN FOR MY FLAIR, HAIR AND SKILL, I'VE PLAYED FOR BARCELONA AND PSG, AND I LOVE DOING TRICKS ON THE PITCH.

WHO AM I?

_____

I'M A YOUNG TALENT FROM SCANDINAVIA, I BROKE NUMEROUS SCORING RECORDS IN EUROPE, AND MY FATHER WAS ALSO A PROFESSIONAL SOCCER PLAYER. I'M KNOWN FOR MY HEIGHT AND GOAL-SCORING ABILITY.

WHO AM I?

_____

I'M KNOWN FOR MY INCREDIBLE WORK RATE IN MIDFIELD, AND I'VE WON THE WORLD CUP, CHAMPIONS LEAGUE, AND PREMIER LEAGUE. DESPITE MY QUIET PERSONALITY, I'M A GIANT ON THE PITCH.

WHO AM I?

_____

# SUDOKU #2

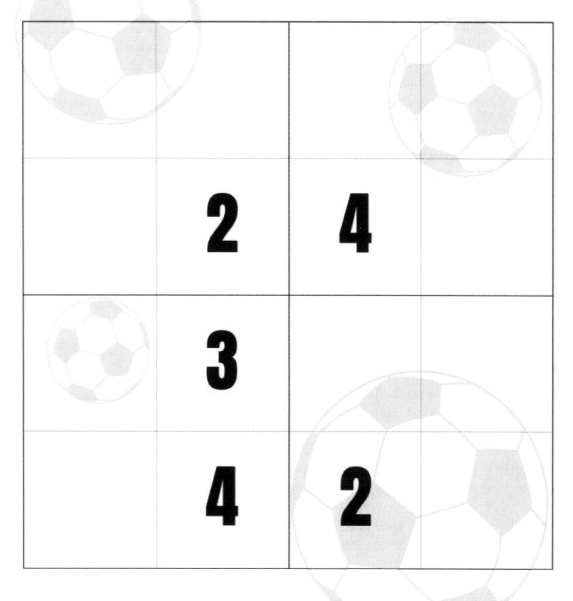

# DESIGN YOUR SOCCER CLEATS

# MAZE #5

# SOCCER FACTS #3

TORONTO FC BECAME THE FIRST MLS TEAM TO WIN THE "TREBLE" IN 2017. THIS MEANS THEY WON THREE MAJOR TROPHIES IN ONE SEASON: THE MLS CUP, THE SUPPORTERS' SHIELD (BEST REGULAR-SEASON RECORD), AND THE CANADIAN CHAMPIONSHIP.

N 2007, MLS INTRODUCED THE DESIGNATED PLAYER RULE TO ALLOW TEAMS TO SIGN HIGH-PROFILE PLAYERS WITHOUT BREAKING THEIR SALARY CAP.

GARETH BARRY HOLDS THE RECORD FOR THE MOST APPEARANCES IN THE ENHLISH PREMIER LEAGUE HISTORY, HAVING PLAYED IN 653 MATCHES DURING HIS CAREER.

# WORD SCRAMBLE #3

**CAN YOU GUESS THE COUNTRY.**

SNAPI

_____

GUOLAPRT

_____

IBAZLR

_____

AANGH

_____

CIOMEX

_____

# COLORING PAGE

# COPY THE DRAWING #3

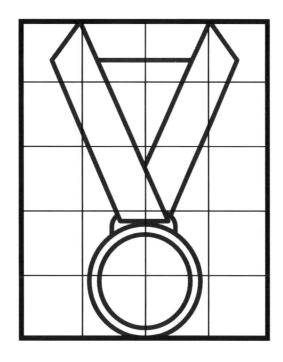

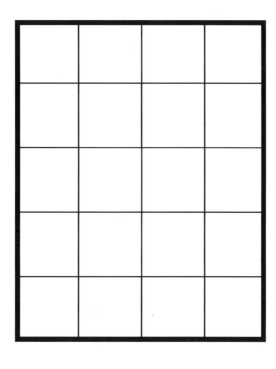

# HISTORY OF SOCCER #2

THE FIFA WORLD CUP TROPHY IS ONE OF THE MOST RECOGNIZED SPORTS TROPHIES IN THE WORLD, MADE OF 18-KARAT GOLD AND REPRESENTS THE HIGHEST ACHIEVEMENT IN SOCCER.

THE 1950 WORLD CUP MATCH BETWEEN BRAZIL AND URUGUAY HOLDS THE RECORD FOR THE LARGEST ATTENDANCE AT ANY SOCCER MATCH, WITH AROUND 200,000 SPECTATORS.

THE TACTIC OF PASSING THE BALL IN A TRIANGLE PATTERN WAS INTRODUCED BY THE HUNGARIANS DURING THE 1950S, REVOLUTIONIZING HOW THE GAME WAS PLAYED.

THE FIRST EVER INTERNATIONAL SOCCER MATCH WAS PLAYED BETWEEN SCOTLAND AND ENGLAND IN 1872. THE MATCH ENDED IN A 0-0 DRAW.

THE CLASSIC BLACK AND WHITE SOCCER DESIGN WAS CREATED FOR THE 1970 FIFA WORLD CUP TO IMPROVE TV VISIBILITY. IT'S CALLED THE TELSTAR.

# DESIGN A SOCCER BALL

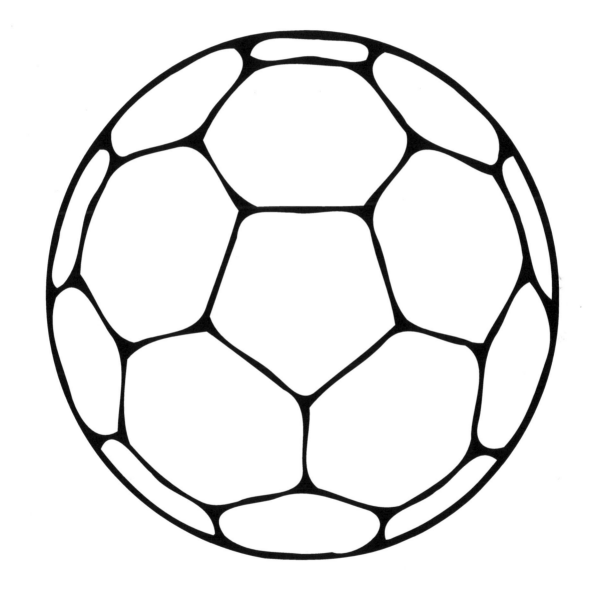

# MAZE #6

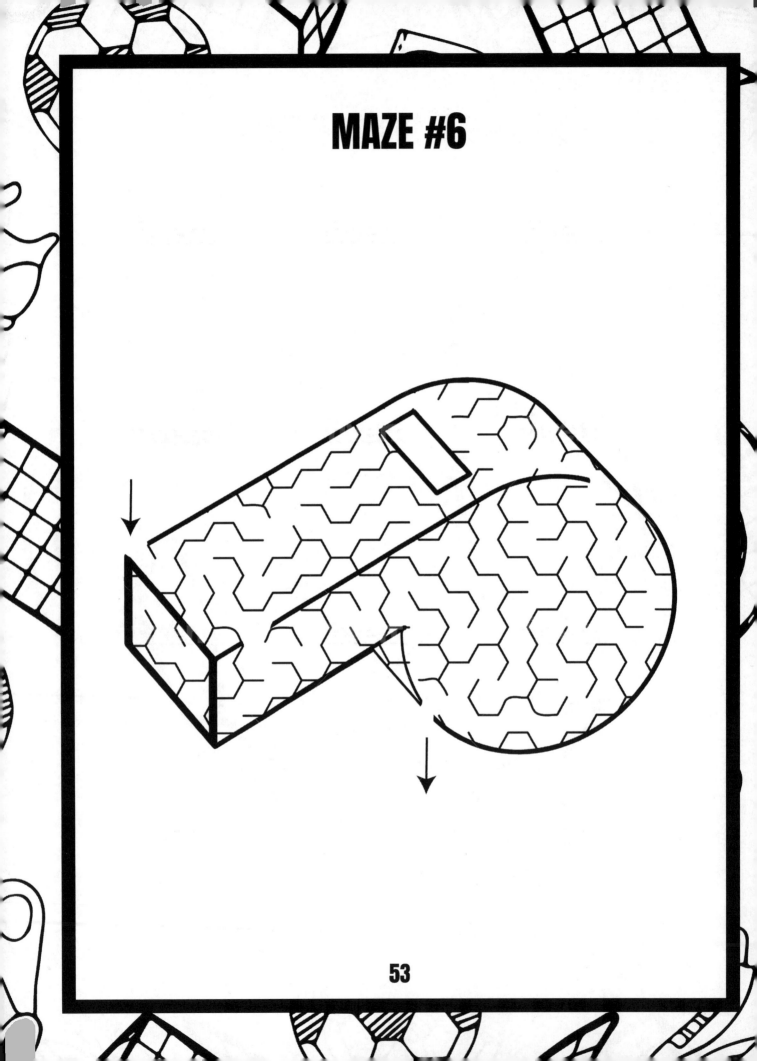

# WORD SEARCH #3

```
I T W D B V P M I D V B Z D I C
E Q T B L V V M J A R K I V O X
B Q C R Q K K M R U M A E U E P
K Y P P A S Q U B W J K F C S J
L Y S R Y I A U P M M G F T X M
B W Z C O H N R K I C K O F F R
W A D B E C E I P C D J G C F X
X N C Z C F P O N P K Z Y P H A
X J M A S U L K L G S Z U P J Z
O V N N D E R E F E R E E K L O
I D A N V E D T P I H X M I I L
J R T Z X Y M L O C T U G X N Z
T L J T Q O J Y G G H M Y Q E Z
M P Z L U L W F G M T Y J T U G
P S S U P P O R T E R S M B P O
V L W D G G Z F S W O T O N S A
```

ACADEMY                    DRAFT
KICKOFF                    LINEUP
REFEREE                    SUPPORTERS
TRAINING                   TRANSFER

# COLORING PAGE

# NAME 10 PLAYERS STARTING WITH A

1. _____

2. _____

3. _____

4. _____

5. _____

6. _____

7. _____

8. _____

9. _____

10. _____

# YOUR FAVOURITE POSITION

. MY FAVORITE POSITION

POSITION NAME: _____
(EXAMPLES: GOALKEEPER, DEFENDER, MIDFIELDER, FORWARD)

2. WHY I LIKE THIS POSITION

WHAT MAKES THIS POSITION SPECIAL: _____
WHAT I ENJOY MOST ABOUT THIS POSITION: _____

3. SKILLS NEEDED FOR THIS POSITION

BEST SKILLS FOR THIS POSITION:

1._____
2._____
3._____

4. FAMOUS PLAYERS WHO PLAY IN THIS POSITION

PLAYER 1: _____
PLAYER 2: _____
PLAYER 3: _____

5. MY ROLE IN THIS POSITION

WHAT I DO TO HELP MY TEAM IN THIS POSITION: _____
MY FAVORITE MEMORY PLAYING IN THIS POSITION: _____

# GUESS THE FLAG #2

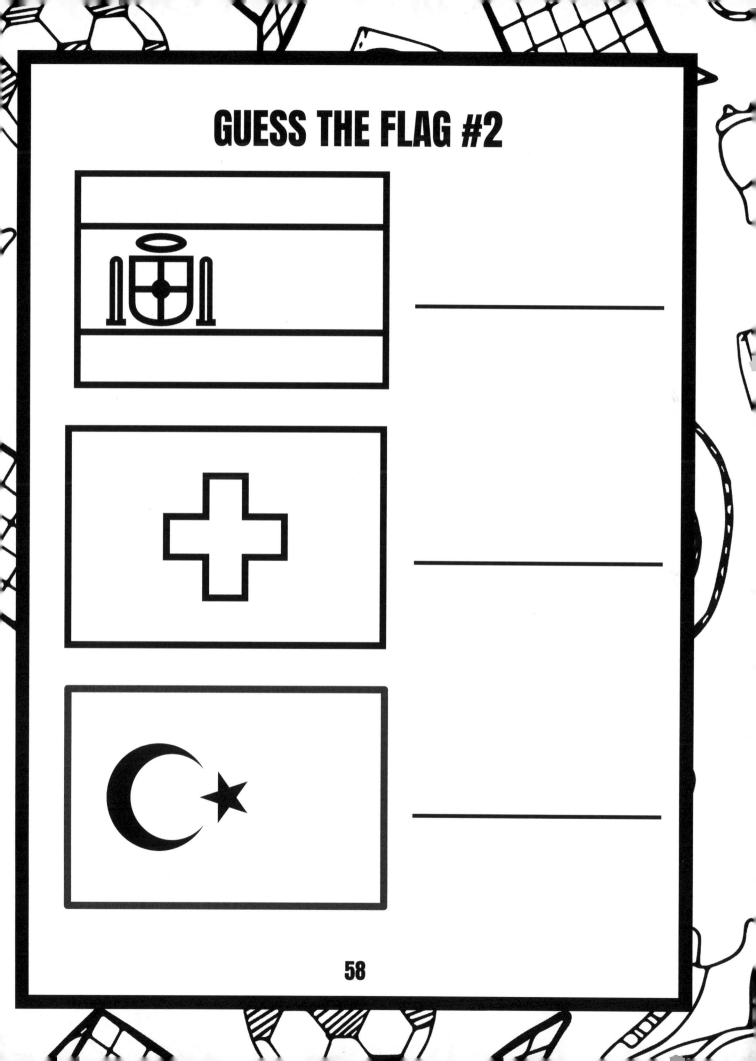

_____

_____

_____

# WORD SCRAMBLE #4

## CAN YOU GUESS THE SOCCER PLAYER?

**AHANDAL** _____

**RGDROOI** _____

**OKANLOM** _____

**MICMIHK** _____

**AERMPL** _____

# RIDDLES #4

I'M A BELGIAN MIDFIELDER KNOWN FOR MY VISION AND PASSING ABILITY. I PLAY FOR ONE OF THE TOP TEAMS IN THE PREMIER LEAGUE AND HAVE WON MULTIPLE LEAGUE TITLES.

### WHO AM I?

_____

I'M A BRAZILIAN WINGER WHO LOVES TO DRIBBLE PAST DEFENDERS. I CURRENTLY PLAY IN SPAIN AND HELPED MY TEAM WIN THE CHAMPIONS LEAGUE WITH CRUCIAL GOALS.

### WHO AM I?

_____

I'M A CANADIAN FULLBACK KNOWN FOR MY SPEED AND ATTACKING CONTRIBUTIONS. I'VE WON MULTIPLE BUNDESLIGA TITLES AND A CHAMPIONS LEAGUE WITH MY GERMAN CLUB.

### WHO AM I?

_____

# SOCCER TACTICS #2

### SET UP YOUR TEAM TO SCORE FROM A WIDE FREE KICK USING 'X' AS YOUR PLAYERS.

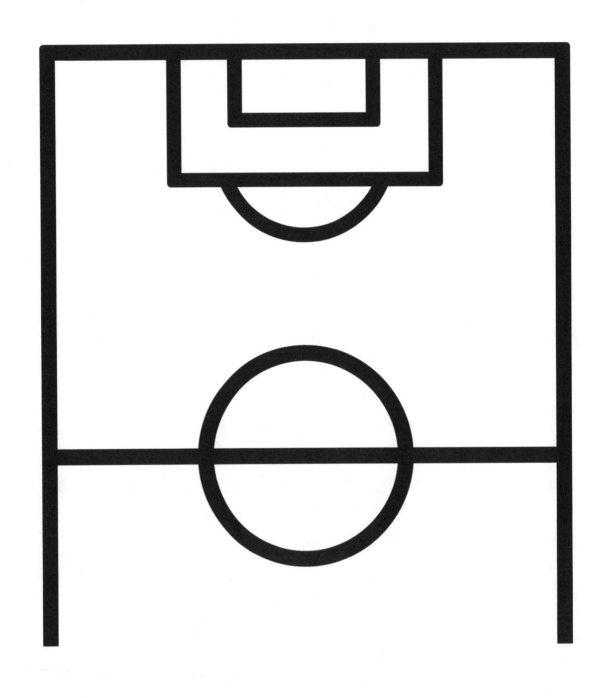

# SOCCER FACTS #4

WONDOLOWSKI IS THE ALL-TIME LEADING GOAL SCORER IN MLS HISTORY WITH 171 GOALS. HE PLAYED THE MAJORITY OF HIS CAREER WITH THE SAN JOSE EARTHQUAKES AND BECAME KNOWN FOR HIS GOAL-SCORING CONSISTENCY OVER MANY SEASONS.

LANDON DONOVAN HOLDS THE RECORD FOR THE MOST ASSISTS IN MLS HISTORY, WITH 136 ASSISTS. HE IS WIDELY REGARDED AS ONE OF THE BEST AMERICAN SOCCER PLAYERS OF ALL TIME AND WAS A KEY PLAYER FOR LA GALAXY.

FREDDY ADU BECAME THE YOUNGEST PLAYER TO EVER SCORE IN AN MLS MATCH AT THE AGE OF 14 YEARS AND 320 DAYS IN 2004 WHILE PLAYING FOR D.C. UNITED.

# COLORING PAGE

# YOUR FAVOURITE TEAM

## CHOOSE A TEAM OF
## YOUR FAVOURITE PLAYERS.

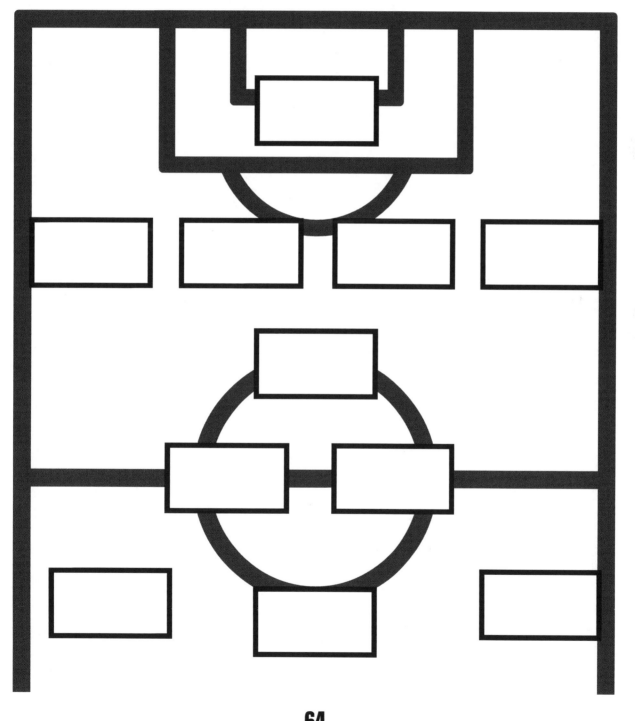

# SPOT THE DIFFERENCE #3

## SPOT THE 3 DIFFERENCES

# WOULD YOU RATHER #4

WOULD YOU RATHER DRIBBLE LIKE MESSI OR SCORE GOALS LIKE RONALDO?

WOULD YOU RATHER PLAY WITH THE CREATIVITY OF NEYMAR OR THE WORK RATE OF N'GOLO KANTÉ?

WOULD YOU RATHER HAVE THE LEADERSHIP QUALITIES OF SERGIO RAMOS OR THE PLAYMAKING ABILITY OF LUKA MODRIĆ?

WOULD YOU RATHER HAVE THE PASSING VISION OF KEVIN DE BRUYNE OR TONI KROOS?

# SUDOKU #3

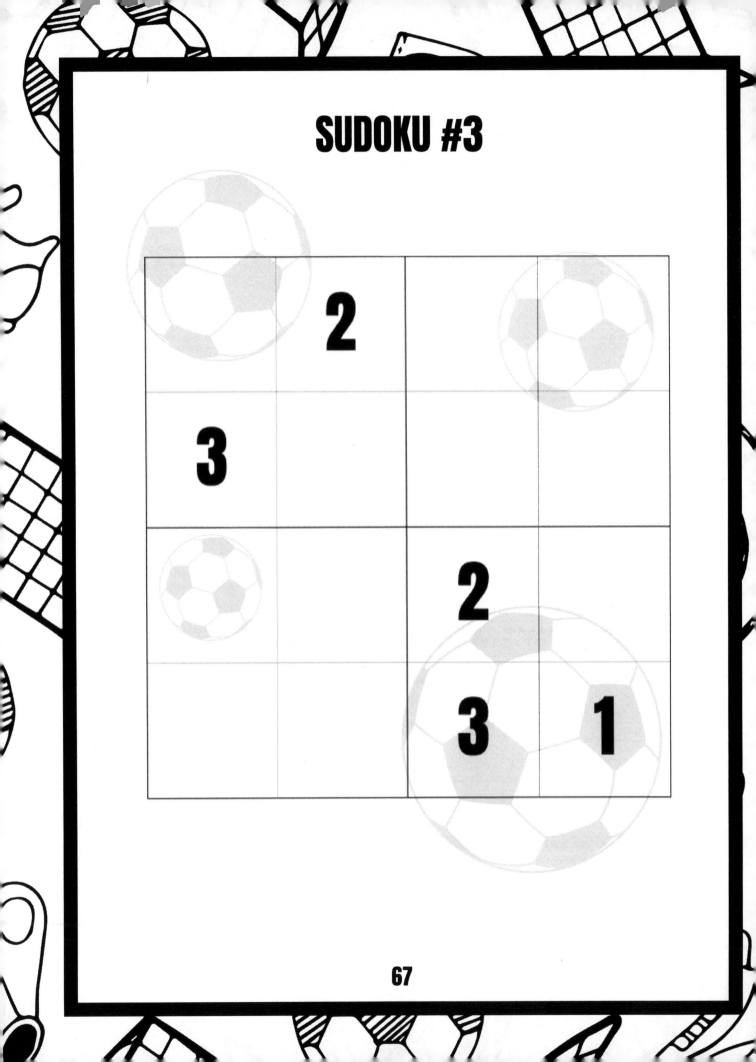

# MAZE #7

# DESIGN YOUR SOCCER LOGO

# COPY THE DRAWING #4

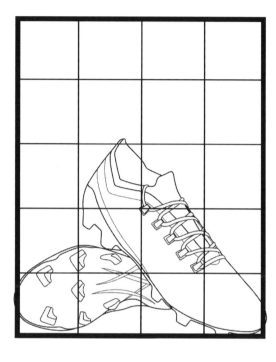

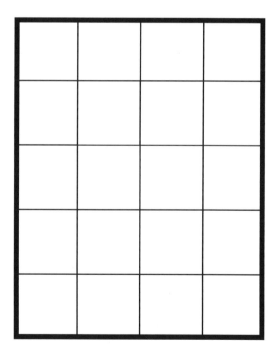

# NAME 10 TEAMS STARTING WITH C

1. _____

2. _____

3. _____

4. _____

5. _____

6. _____

7. _____

8. _____

9. _____

10. _____

# SOCCER TACTICS #3

## SET UP YOUR TEAM TO DEFEND A CORNER USING 'X' AS YOUR PLAYERS.

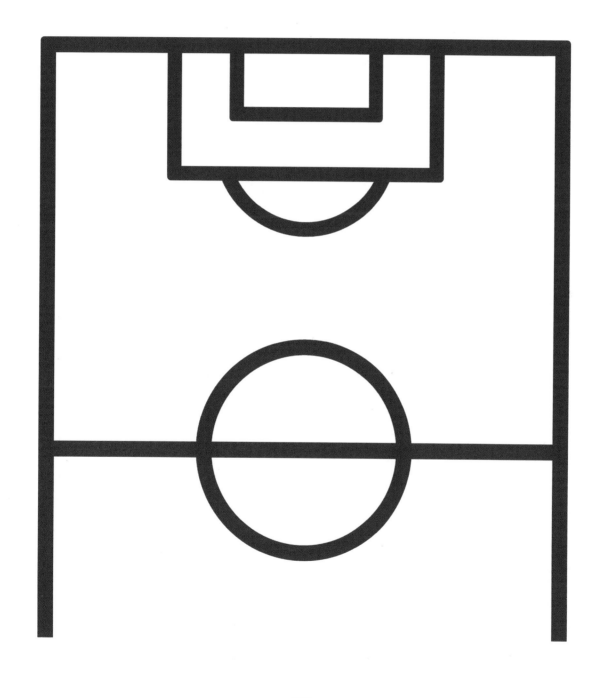

# WORD SEARCH #4

```
G Z O Q I I F J N X Y I P I O M
L R T B G Q L J R I M S V L D T
U Q G B E I W X K R K P I Q V Z
A J Q H H F H X O G F Y O A U M
Y D E L S I I F L D A F U D Q F
D Z X U Z E I G X B A D G E E N
R D R L T N A U D T I J Q I H O
F H I S U H S M J R Y V U T P Z
K A X Z Q C M U Q B I B S F P U
F T Z S H U R X X U U B H K M B
C T P A S S I S T L N E B H C F
O R A A A J K W C Z H F R L I S
O I L E S N L O W S E E H J E N
Q C O Q M S Y B K Y A A E T T Y
H K L E T H S M Q V Y E P E H N
D J Q T I C A P T A I N C Y J R
```

ASSIST

CAPTAINCY

DRIBBLE

PASS

BADGE

CLUB

HATTRICK

UNIFORM

# YOUR ULTIMATE NATIONAL TEAM PLAYER

### NAME YOUR ULTIMATE PLAYER FOR YOUR NATIONAL TEAM IN EACH BOX

INTELLIGENCE

HEADING

LEADER

STRENGTH

SPEED

ENDURANCE

SHOOTING

# MAZE #8

# GUESS THE FLAG #3

_____

_____

_____

# SOCCER MATHS #2

A TEAM SCORES 5 GOALS IN THEIR FIRST MATCH, 3 GOALS IN THEIR SECOND MATCH, AND DOUBLES THEIR SECOND MATCH SCORE IN THEIR THIRD MATCH. HOW MANY GOALS DID THEY SCORE IN TOTAL OVER THE THREE MATCHES?

_____

A SOCCER PLAYER TAKES 9 SHOTS AT GOAL IN ONE GAME AND SCORES WITH 1/3 OF THEM. IN THE NEXT GAME, THEY TAKE 12 SHOTS AND SCORE WITH 1/4 OF THEM. HOW MANY GOALS DID THEY SCORE IN TOTAL OVER THE TWO GAMES?

_____

THERE ARE 18 PLAYERS ON A SOCCER TEAM, AND EACH PLAYER DRINKS 2 BOTTLES OF WATER PER GAME. IF THE TEAM PLAYS 5 GAMES IN A WEEK, HOW MANY BOTTLES OF WATER DO THEY DRINK IN TOTAL?

_____

# COLORING PAGE

# 2025 PREDICTIONS

WIN MLS CUP

_____

WIN LA LIGA

_____

WIN BUNDESLIGA

_____

WIN THE PREMIER LEAGUE

_____

MOST GOALS

_____

MOST ASSISTS

_____

WIN BALLON D'OR

_____

# WORD SCRAMBLE #5

**CAN YOU GUESS THE SOCCER STADIUM?**

WBYEMLE

_____

EHADIT

_____

INALAZL ERNAA

_____

PRAC EDS PERSINC

_____

DER LUBL AAERN

_____

# SOCCER FACTS #5

MIKE GRELLA SCORED THE FASTEST GOAL IN MLS HISTORY, JUST 7 SECONDS INTO A MATCH FOR THE NEW YORK RED BULLS AGAINST THE PHILADELPHIA UNION IN 2015.

LA GALAXY HOLDS THE RECORD FOR THE MOST MLS CUP TITLES, WITH 5 CHAMPIONSHIPS (2002, 2005, 2011, 2012, AND 2014). THEY ARE ONE OF THE MOST SUCCESSFUL CLUBS IN LEAGUE HISTORY.

THE COLUMBUS CREW HOLDS THE RECORD FOR THE LONGEST UNBEATEN STREAK IN MLS HISTORY, GOING 19 GAMES WITHOUT A LOSS DURING THE 2004 SEASON.

# RIDDLES #5

I'M THE HOME OF A CLUB THAT WEARS RED, BUT MY HISTORY IS PAINTED IN EUROPEAN GLORY. I'M LOCATED IN A CITY KNOWN FOR MUSIC, AMOUS DOCKS AND THE SONG "YOU'LL NEVER WALK ALONE".

## WHAT STADIUM AM I?

_____

I'M LOCATED IN GERMANY, AND MY FANS CREATE ONE OF THE MOST INTIMIDATING ATMOSPHERES IN SOCCER. MY ICONIC YELLOW WALL IS KNOWN FOR ITS PASSIONATE SUPPORT.

## WHAT STADIUM AM I?

_____

I'M IN ONE OF THE COLDEST COUNTRIES TO HOST THE WORLD CUP. MY RETRACTABLE ROOF AND IMPRESSIVE DESIGN MAKE ME A LANDMARK. I HOSTED THE FINAL OF THE 2018 WORLD CUP.

## WHAT STADIUM AM I?

_____

# SPOT THE DIFFERENCE #4

## SPOT THE 3 DIFFERENCES.

# WOULD YOU RATHER #5

WOULD YOU RATHER PLAY AT THE HISTORIC CAMP NOU (BARCA) OR THE SANTIAGO BERNABEU (REAL MADRID)?

WOULD YOU RATHER PLAY FOR LA GALAXY OR LOS ANGELES FC?

WOULD YOU RATHER EXPERIENCE THE ATMOSPHERE OF ANFIELD (LIVERPOOL) OR THE ELECTRIC CROWD AT SIGNAL IDUNA PARK (BORUSSIA DORTMUND)?

WOULD YOU RATHER PLAY A CUP FINAL AT WEMBLEY STADIUM (LONDON) OR THE MARACANÃ (RIO DE JANEIRO)?

# COLORING PAGE

# DESIGN YOUR OWN FLAG

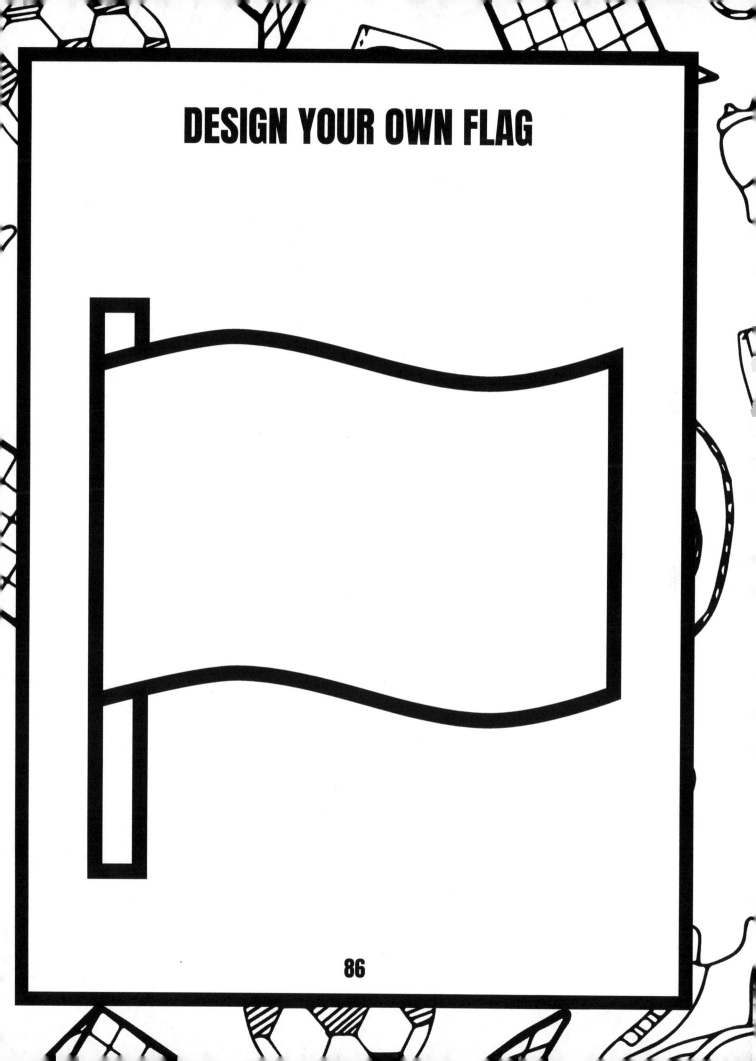

# MAZE #9

# BINGO

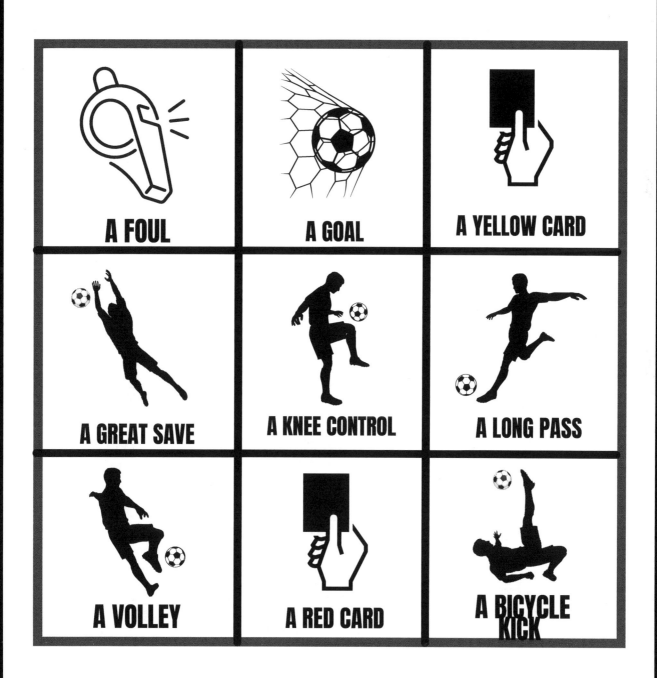

A FOUL

A GOAL

A YELLOW CARD

A GREAT SAVE

A KNEE CONTROL

A LONG PASS

A VOLLEY

A RED CARD

A BICYCLE KICK

# SUDOKU #4

# COPY THE DRAWING #5

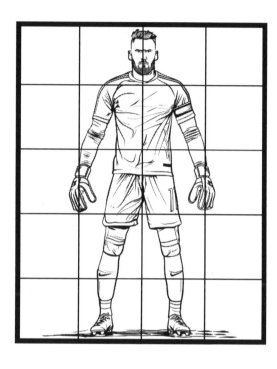

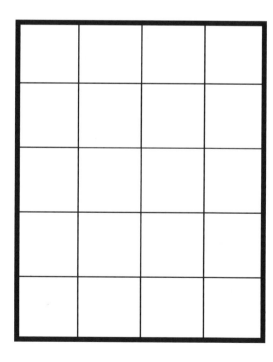

# SOCCER COMIC

# SOCCER COMIC

# MAZE #10

# SOCCER MATHS #3

1. IN A SOCCER LEAGUE, EACH TEAM PLAYS 2 MATCHES AGAINST EVERY OTHER TEAM. IF THERE ARE 8 TEAMS IN THE LEAGUE, HOW MANY TOTAL MATCHES ARE PLAYED?

_____

2. A SOCCER STADIUM HAS 50,000 SEATS. IF 80% OF THE SEATS ARE SOLD FOR A MATCH, HOW MANY SEATS REMAIN EMPTY?

_____

3. A PLAYER SCORES 3 GOALS IN EVERY 4 MATCHES. IF THEY PLAY 20 MATCHES IN A SEASON, HOW MANY GOALS WILL THEY SCORE?

_____

4. IN A TOURNAMENT, THERE ARE 16 TEAMS, AND EACH TEAM SCORES AN AVERAGE OF 2 GOALS PER GAME. IF EACH TEAM PLAYS 3 MATCHES, HOW MANY TOTAL GOALS ARE SCORED IN THE TOURNAMENT?

_____

5. A SOCCER PLAYER PLAYS 30 MATCHES IN A SEASON. IN 40% OF THE MATCHES, THEY SCORE AT LEAST ONE GOAL. HOW MANY MATCHES DID THEY SCORE IN?

_____

# WORD SEARCH #5

```
C D L V I B Z A K O O Y P F U Y
P Q L V S P O N S O R S H I P O
C U D R O I G Q Z H U V I V I W
W J N P P G B T O T H Q H W E G
R P B F V J E H U A P D E E N M
I G O S X L K R D C Y Y A A X P
V C U M I N G O P K T M D G C S
A Z N H S T A W J L C H E V G T
L R L P A Y W I A E E T R L V B
R Z F G O N C N S Y M E P V M X
Y D X M O E E H B W L V Q M L A
W D G G W P A N X G E V J Y E V
R A S E T P I E C E L E H F D P
U V R I J X U S Q S B U P A N M
O A I G Q W I D J U N S X E Y Z
S H J X W X L S U X S H S F R U
```

HEADER

RIVALRY

SPONSORSHIP

TACKLE

PENALTY

SET PIECE

SWEEPER

THROW IN

# HISTORY OF SOCCER #3

THE FIRST LIVE TELEVISED FOOTBALL MATCH WAS A FRIENDLY MATCH BETWEEN ARSENAL'S FIRST TEAM AND THEIR RESERVES IN 1937.

THE PENALTY KICK WAS INTRODUCED IN 1891 AFTER A SUGGESTION BY IRISH GOALKEEPER WILLIAM MCCRUM IN 1890, DUE TO INCREASING INCIDENTS OF HANDLING THE BALL TO PREVENT GOALS.

GOALKEEPERS STARTED WEARING GLOVES IN THE 1970S FOR BETTER GRIP AND PROTECTION, ALTHOUGH SOME GOALIES EXPERIMENTED WITH VARIOUS TYPES OF HAND PROTECTION MUCH EARLIER.

THE FASTEST GOAL IN PROFESSIONAL SOCCER HISTORY WAS SCORED JUST 2.8 SECONDS AFTER KICKOFF BY NAWAF AL-ABED OF SAUDI ARABIA IN 2009.

SUBSTITUTIONS WERE FIRST ALLOWED IN ENGLISH SOCCER IN 1965. BEFORE THEN, INJURED PLAYERS HAD TO PLAY ON OR LEAVE THEIR TEAM SHORT-HANDED.

# SPOT THE DIFFERENCE #5

## SPOT THE 3 DIFFERENCES

# COLORING PAGE

# NAME 10 PLAYERS STARTING WITH P

1. _____

2. _____

3. _____

4. _____

5. _____

6. _____

7. _____

8. _____

9. _____

10. _____

# SUDOKU #5

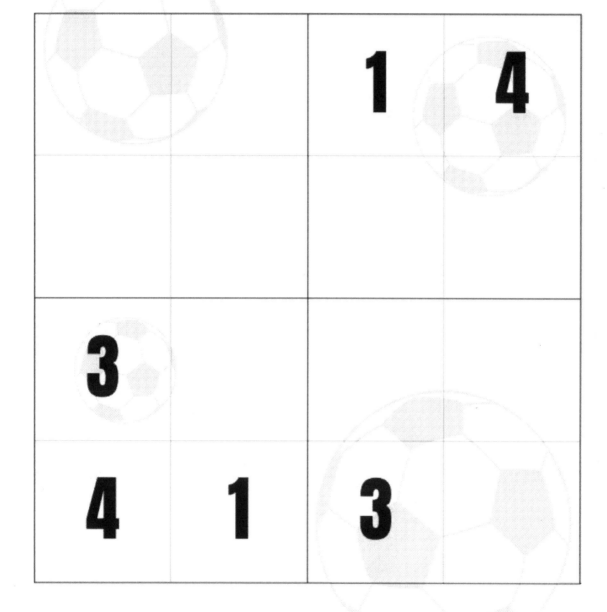

# YOUR THE MANAGER #2

## CHOOSE YOUR TEAM TO FACE A TECHNICAL, POSSESSION-BASED TEAM.

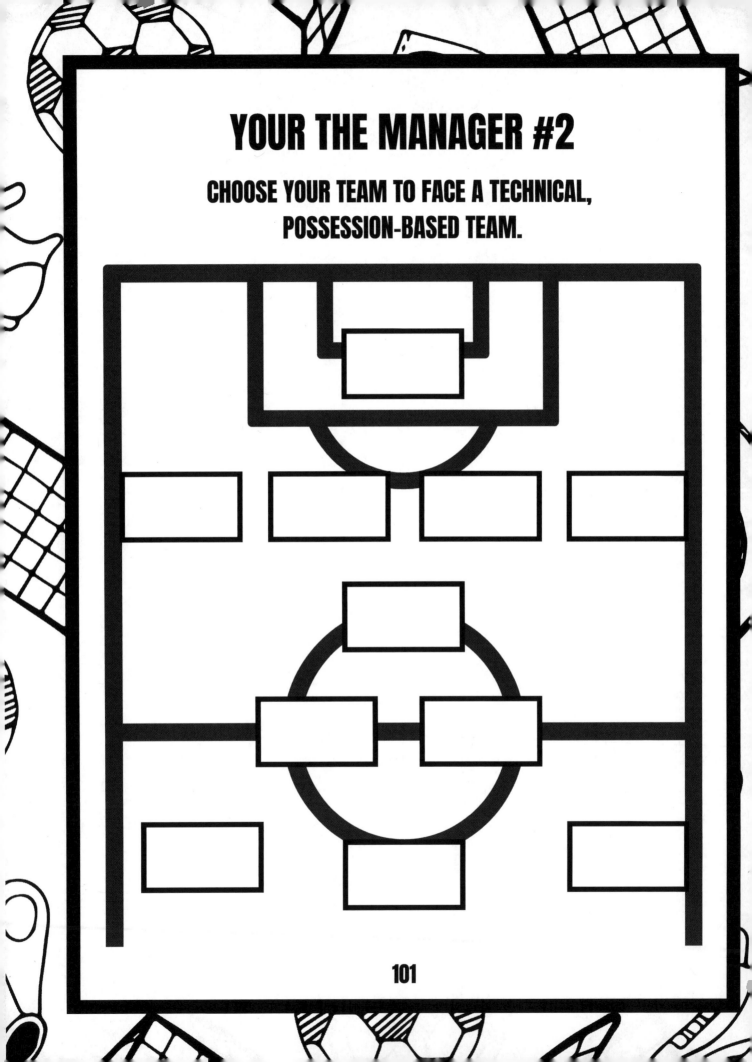

# SOLUTIONS

# SUDOKU

| 3 | 2 | 1 | 4 |
|---|---|---|---|
| 1 | 4 | 2 | 3 |
| 2 | 3 | 4 | 1 |
| 4 | 1 | 3 | 2 |

| 4 | 1 | 3 | 2 |
|---|---|---|---|
| 3 | 2 | 4 | 1 |
| 2 | 3 | 1 | 4 |
| 1 | 4 | 2 | 3 |

| 4 | 2 | 1 | 3 |
|---|---|---|---|
| 3 | 1 | 4 | 2 |
| 1 | 3 | 2 | 4 |
| 2 | 4 | 3 | 1 |

| 2 | 4 | 3 | 1 |
|---|---|---|---|
| 3 | 1 | 4 | 2 |
| 4 | 2 | 1 | 3 |
| 1 | 3 | 2 | 4 |

# SUDOKU

#5

| | | | |
|---|---|---|---|
| 2 | 3 | 1 | 4 |
| 1 | 4 | 2 | 3 |
| 3 | 2 | 4 | 1 |
| 4 | 1 | 3 | 2 |

# WORD SEARCH

### Puzzle #1 - Solution

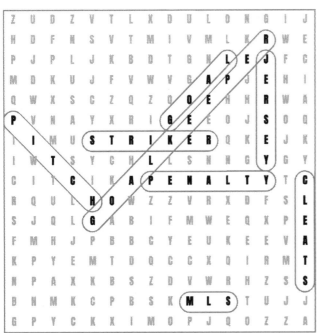

### Puzzle #2 - Solution

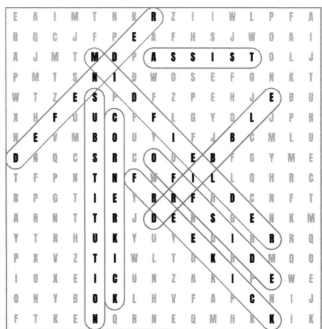

### Puzzle #3 - Solution

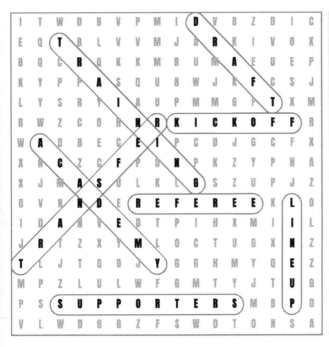

### Puzzle #4 - Solution

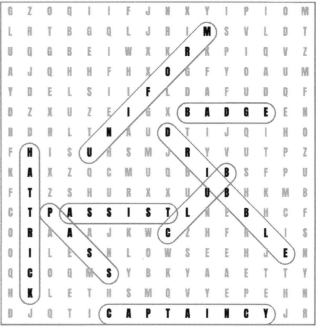

# WORD SEARCH

## Puzzle #5 - Solution

Found words: SPONSORSHIP, THROWIN, TACKLE, HEADER, RIVALRY, SETPIECE, GOALKEEPER

# SPOT THE DIFFERENCE

### #1

### #2

### #3

### #4

# SPOT THE DIFFERENCE

#5

# SOCCER MATHS

**#1**

1. ANSWER: ◈ = 4 (6 + 6 + ◈ = 16; 12 + ◈ = 16, SO ◈ = 4)

2. ANSWER: ▷ = 6 (8 + 8 + ▷ + ▷ = 28; 16 + 2▷ = 28, SO 2▷ = 12, AND ▷ = 6).

3. ANSWER:   = 10 (5 + 7 +   = 22; 12 +   = 22, SO   = 10).

**#2**

1.ANSWER: 16 GOALS (5 + 3 + (3 X 2) = 5 + 3 + 6 = 14 GOALS).

2.ANSWER: 5 GOALS (1/3 OF 9 = 3 GOALS, 1/4 OF 12 = 3 GOALS; TOTAL = 3 + 3 = 6 GOALS).

3. ANSWER: 180 BOTTLES (18 PLAYERS X 2 BOTTLES X 5 GAMES = 180 BOTTLES).

**#3**

1.ANSWER: 56 MATCHES (EACH TEAM PLAYS 7 OTHER TEAMS TWICE: 8 X 7 = 56)

2. ANSWER: 10,000 SEATS (20% OF 50,000 = 10,000)

3. ANSWER: 15 GOALS (3 GOALS PER 4 MATCHES, SO 20 MATCHES ÷ 4 = 5; 5 × 3 = 15)

4. IANSWER: 96 GOALS (16 TEAMS X 2 GOALS X 3 MATCHES = 96).

5. ANSWER: 12 MATCHES (40% OF 30 = 12).

# WORD SCRAMBLE

## #1

| | |
|---|---|
| YESEJR | JERSEY |
| SCSKO | SOCKS |
| REGA | GEAR |
| TSORHS | SHORTS |
| ASTELC | CLEATS |

## #2

| | |
|---|---|
| ANM INUDET | MAN UNITED |
| LEESAHC | CHELSEA |
| LSAARNE | ARSENAL |
| IERTN IMIAM CF | INTER MIAMI CF |
| ERAL RMIDDA | REAL MADRID |

## #3

| | |
|---|---|
| SNAPI | SPAIN |
| GUOLAPRT | PORTUGAL |
| IBAZLR | BRAZIL |
| AANGH | GHANA |
| CIOMEX | MEXICO |

## #4

| | |
|---|---|
| AHANDAL | HAALAND |
| RGDROOI | RODRIGO |
| OKANLOM | LOOKMAN |
| MICMIHK | KIMMICH |
| AERMPL | PALMER |

## #5

| | |
|---|---|
| WBYEMLE | WEMBLEY |
| EHADIT | ETIHAD |
| INALAZL ERNAA | ALLIANZ ARENA |
| PRAC EDS PERSINC | PARC DES PRINCES |
| DER LUBL AAERN | RED BULL ARENA |

110

# RIDDLES

### #1

I RUN UP AND DOWN
THE FIELD ALL DAY,
BLOWING MY WHISTLE
TO CONTROL THE PLAY.

WHO AM I?

A REFEREE.

I PROTECT YOUR LEGS
DURING THE GAME, SO
YOU DON'T FEEL THE
KICK OR THE PAIN.

WHAT AM I?

SHIN GUARDS

I'M LACED UP TIGHT
AND HELP YOU RUN
FAST, I'M WORN ON
YOUR FEET, AND I'M
BUILT TO LAST.

WHAT AM I?

SOCCER CLEATS

### #2

I'M AN ENGLISH FORWARD
WHO PLAYS IN GERMANY, I'VE
WON MULTIPLE PREMIER
LEAGUE GOLDEN BOOTS.

WHO AM I?

HARRY KANE

I'M A POLISH STRIKER KNOWN
FOR SCORING LOTS OF GOALS,
I'VE PLAYED FOR BAYERN
MUNICH AND BARCELONA.

WHO AM I?

LEWANDOWSKI

I'M AN EGYPTIAN FORWARD
WITH AMAZING GOAL-SCORING
SKILLS, I'VE WON THE
PREMIER LEAGUE AND
CHAMPIONS LEAGUE WITH
LIVERPOOL.

WHO AM I?

SALAH

### #3

I'M A BRAZILIAN FORWARD KNOWN
FOR MY FLAIR, HAIR AND SKILL, I'VE
PLAYED FOR BARCELONA AND PSG,
AND I LOVE DOING TRICKS ON
THE PITCH.

WHO AM I?

NEYMAR JR

I'M A YOUNG TALENT FROM
SCANDINAVIA, I BROKE NUMEROUS
SCORING RECORDS IN EUROPE, AND
MY FATHER WAS ALSO A
PROFESSIONAL SOCCER PLAYER. I'M
KNOWN FOR MY HEIGHT AND GOAL-
SCORING ABILITY.

WHO AM I?

ERLING HAALAND

I'M KNOWN FOR MY INCREDIBLE
WORK RATE IN MIDFIELD, AND
I'VE WON THE WORLD CUP,
CHAMPIONS LEAGUE, AND
PREMIER LEAGUE. DESPITE MY
QUIET PERSONALITY, I'M A GIANT
ON THE PITCH.

WHO AM I?

N'GOLO KANTÉ

# RIDDLES

## #4

I'M A BELGIAN MIDFIELDER KNOWN FOR MY VISION AND PASSING ABILITY. I PLAY FOR ONE OF THE TOP TEAMS IN THE PREMIER LEAGUE AND HAVE WON MULTIPLE LEAGUE TITLES.

WHO AM I?

KEVIN DE BRUYNE

I'M A BRAZILIAN WINGER WHO LOVES TO DRIBBLE PAST DEFENDERS. I CURRENTLY PLAY IN SPAIN AND HELPED MY TEAM WIN THE CHAMPIONS LEAGUE WITH CRUCIAL GOALS.

WHO AM I?

VINÍCIUS JÚNIOR

I'M A CANADIAN FULLBACK KNOWN FOR MY SPEED AND ATTACKING CONTRIBUTIONS. I'VE WON MULTIPLE BUNDESLIGA TITLES AND A CHAMPIONS LEAGUE WITH MY GERMAN CLUB.

WHO AM I?

ALPHONSO DAVIES

## #5

I'M THE HOME OF A CLUB THAT WEARS RED, BUT MY HISTORY IS PAINTED IN EUROPEAN GLORY. I'M LOCATED IN A CITY KNOWN FOR MUSIC, AMOUS DOCKS AND THE SONG "YOU'LL NEVER WALK ALONE".

WHAT STADIUM AM I?

ANFIELD

'M LOCATED IN GERMANY, AND MY FANS CREATE ONE OF THE MOST INTIMIDATING ATMOSPHERES IN SOCCER. MY ICONIC YELLOW WALL IS KNOWN FOR ITS PASSIONATE SUPPORT.

WHAT STADIUM AM I?

SIGNAL IDUNA PARK

'M IN ONE OF THE COLDEST COUNTRIES TO HOST THE WORLD CUP. MY RETRACTABLE ROOF AND IMPRESSIVE DESIGN MAKE ME A LANDMARK. I HOSTED THE FINAL OF THE 2018 WORLD CUP.

WHAT STADIUM AM I?

LUZHNIKI STADIUM (MOSCOW)

# GUESS THE FLAG

## #1

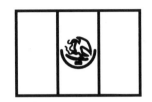 MEXICO

 BRAZIL

 ARGENTINA

## #2

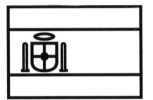 SPAIN

 SWITZERLAND

 TURKEY

## #3

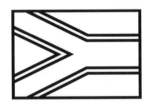 SOUTH AFRICA

 HONDURAS

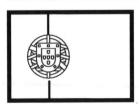 PORTUGAL